RECESSIONAL

also by Jack Robinson

Days and Nights in W12

'Buy this book . . . Then ask yourself: How can I be that imaginative? That perceptive? That concise?' – thefictiondesk.com

RECESSIONAL

JACK ROBINSON

CB*editions*

First published in 2009
by CB editions
146 Percy Road London W12 9QL
www.cbeditions.com

All rights reserved

© Jack Robinson, 2009

The right of Jack Robinson to be identified as author
of this work has been asserted in accordance
with the Copyright, Designs and Patents Act, 1988

Printed in England by Primary Colours, London W3 8DH

ISBN 978–0–9561073–1–2

The lion tamer is up early, walking briskly between the caravans on his way to the cages, hunks of raw meat in the plastic bags he carries. Last night he wowed them: every new trick came off, every fancy routine he'd spent months perfecting, and the audience loved it, bayed for more. As he enters the wagon his prize animal stirs on the floor of its cage and rises to its feet, smelling blood. He puts down the bags and reaches for his key.

'And there's an amazing moment: each day, before the day starts, before the market opens, before the bidding begins, there's a moment of confusion: the money is silent, it hasn't yet spoken. Its decisions are withheld, poised, perched, ready.'
   – Wallace Shawn, *The Fever* (1990)

This is my father driving in the 1940s, before I was born. He left school at fourteen to work in an iron foundry his own father had helped establish; he eventually became joint managing director. We had a comfortable life without my mother having to work; single-income households were common then. He liked cars: I remember waiting at the front-room window one afternoon, when I was four or five years old, to see him arrive home in a brand-new olive-green Riley. Fifty years on from pressing my face against that window, I know that at no time has my own income been sufficient to raise a family in similar comfort, nor will I ever own a brand-new car; and my children will, if they go to college, be already mired in debt before they even begin to earn their own money. The car I can do without, but strip away the mirage of affluence offered by cheap credit and it's clear that in my generation, despite the huge increase in productivity enabled by computers, more people have been working for less real money than before; while profits and the pay bundles of CEOs have soared; and imposing a few regulations on the banks is chickenfeed.

... privilege to be with you here tonight and I'd like to thank our sponsors and all those who've worked tirelessly in the background to put on this fine spread but above all I'd like to thank you without whom etc because it's you who have exercised your inalienable right to go out into the world and spend and spend your minimum wages and thanks to the generosity of our sponsors much more besides and it's you young ones especially future of our country heritage etc who have been investing the money that god knows you will one day surely earn (and pay back) on acquiring the skills to put a smile on the face of the economy and broadband for all and scratchcards and never in history this sceptred isle so much choice even the basic box has fifty-five channels and if you can't read the leaflets all you have to do is ring up for a large-print version and jobs too because if you don't have jobs you'll never be able to keep up those repayments however long toil sweat blood tears just look at the figures so it's all your fault really if you choose to ignore your safety and security our paramount concern seatbelts helmets five portions alcohol daily leading by example and sub-indices market green shoots sponsors here not unfortunately tonight service as soon resumed normal will be as ...

'Lo, all our pomp of yesterday
Is one with Nineveh and Tyre!'
 – Rudyard Kipling, 'Recessional'

Nineveh and Tyre – not to mention Antioch, Babylon and Zanadu . . . Far from looking on their works with despair, we join sightseeing tours and queue to gawp at their artefacts at the British Museum: because right now it's we who are winning, we are alive and they are not. We gloat. We preserve ruins because they tell us that we are not yet, for all our idiocies, ruins ourselves. And the best of them – not the tedious imperial arches; I mean the way a line renders a hip-bone, or the otherness of an animal – suggest what we might still be capable of. But the new room at the Bank of England Museum (opening hours 10 a.m. to 5 p.m. Monday to Friday, closed on Bank Holidays) is disappointing: a few printed-off expense accounts and a scale model of a black hole.

Hey presto, abracadabra – the Amazing Pecuniarus. Choose a card, any card. Rabbits from hats, doves from scarves. Give me your savings and I will double them, treble them. Watch me vanish before your very eyes.

'*Walk fast and look worried*'

Exiting the boardroom, is he
(a) sneezing?
(b) sicking up his breakfast while making a dash for the gents?
(b) thinking, Shit, there goes another twenty million?
(c) praying to the Lord Almighty?

This is the house that Jack bought.

This is the mortgage lender from the bank that lent Jack the money to buy his house.

This is banker 1 who lent the mortgage lender money to lend to Jack to buy his house, and thus bought a debt – or rather, looking ahead, an asset, being the rights to the repayment of that debt.

This is banker 2 who borrowed money from banker 3 to buy the debt/asset from banker 1 and a few others besides, and wrapped them up nicely and tied them with a pink ribbon and sold them on to banker 4, who bought them with money borrowed from banker 5 and in turn carried on spreading the joy.

This is the big chief banker who raised interest rates because of inflation.

This is Jack again, whose mortgage payments have risen and who can't keep paying them.

This is Jack's house again, back on sale for less than he paid for it because no one will lend anyone money to buy it – either because they can no longer borrow money to lend or because they don't believe they've a cat's chance in hell of ever getting it back.

These are various bankers who joined in the game but are now in pain because they've stubbed their big toe on a synthetic collateralised debt obligation.

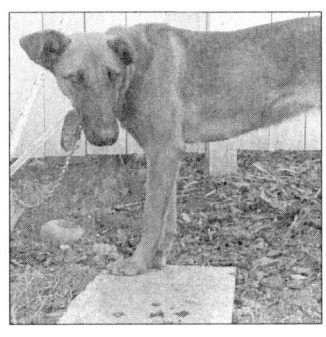

This is Jack's dog, and Jack has a question for him: Why would *anyone* lend money to a guy with a part-time job sweeping out monkey cages in the zoo?

Too easy, says dog. They couldn't lose: their money back plus more, or a house worth more than you'd borrowed in the first place.

But it isn't now, is it? How come I borrowed so *much*?

Good question, says dog. Pour me a whisky. Long story. 1970s to now, wages stay low for the workers, rise for the bosses. How do the workers buy all the stuff getting made? The bosses lend them what they're not paying in wages. The whole place gets run on debt, to the point where household debt becomes higher than the GDP. No one blinks, because this is fine as long as your house keeps going up in value, but when that bubble bursts the shit hits the fan.

Uh-huh, says Jack. Monkey shit, I know that stuff. Why did no one point out that that's what the whole cat's-cradle was built over?

Dog holds out his glass for a refill. Says: Oh, they knew. But when most people are getting what they want, why stop? And the banking stuff, that was all about chasing returns – you give me money, I'll give you back more than you'll get from anyone else, promise. I know about chasing things.

Uh-huh, says Jack. Dog, you know when you pee on a lamp post, sometimes barely a trickle? What's that all about? What's the rate of return?

'One day apes made their grab for power.
Gold seal-rings,
starched shirts,
aromatic Havanas,
feet squashed into patent leather.
Deeply involved in our other pursuits,
we didn't notice . . .'
  – Adam Zagajewski, 'Apes'

'It's easier to rob by setting up a bank than by holding up a bank clerk.' – Brecht

Brecht was a keen smoker of cigars ('And when the earthquakes come, I hope I won't be bitter / And won't let my cigar go out in the gloom'), as were both Karl and Groucho Marx. In 2007 smoking in banks and other public places became illegal in England, but not reckless profiteering. Below is a cigar shop opposite the Bank of England: 'They need a cigar, but they need money as well,' said the owner of his regulars in February 2009.

TOAD: There is a profound and unqualified apology for all the distress that has been caused.

BADGER: Are you personally culpable?

TOAD: What I'm concerned about is that it is just too simple if you want to blame it all on me.

BADGER: Did you personally understand the full complexity of these vehicles that your clever young men were creating?

TOAD: No, I didn't, that's part of the secret of how you manage risk.

BADGER: Do you have any formal banking qualifications?

TOAD: I don't know whether you would call them banking qualifications but I have a degree in law and I qualified as a chartered accountant.

BADGER: Do you think a banking qualification per se is important?

TOAD: (Silence.)

Toad's lines on the left were spoken on 10 February 2009 (in reply to questions from MPs) by Sir Fred Goodwin, former group chief executive of RBS (which in early 2009 posted the biggest loss in UK corporate history; Goodwin took early retirement, with a pension for life of £700,000 a year). Kenneth Grahame wrote *The Wind in the Willows* (1908) – in which Toad is bailed out from various scrapes by kindly others who have a soft spot for this feckless, conceited toff – while working at the Bank of England. Several of Grahame's colleagues kept dogs in the basement and organised dog-fights in the lavatories. In 1903 he was shot at by an intruder named Robinson (no relation), whom the press referred to as a 'Socialist Lunatic'.

The ignorance of the experts concerning the financial products they were using our money to buy is hardly new. James Buchan, in the late 1980s: 'In London and New York I met people who invested fortunes in financial enterprises they simply could not describe or explain. No doubt quite soon, a bank would discover it had lost its capital in those obscure speculations; other banks would fail in sympathy . . .' The politicians were even more ignorant. It's as if for years we've been going with our tummy-aches to doctors who can't tell the difference between a blister and a cancerous tumour. No wonder we're ill.

In shoot-'em-up video games, the low-lives you blast to kingdom come on your way to your highest score aren't *real*, though government health warnings are occasionally issued: these games can be addictive.

Over Afghanistan, the target co-ordinates for laser-guided bombs are shown on screens: pinpoint accuracy, except for the occasional wedding party. Collateral damage. The pilot, high in the sky, neither sees nor feels a thing.

Baudrillard's *The Gulf War Did Not Take Place* (1991) argued that what was presented on TV screens was far removed from the actual events, and that we now take for real what is only spectacle.

Second Life, the virtual world accessible on the net since 2003, offers not an alternative to the actual world but more of the same – buying and selling, mostly – in an environment in which you can choose to be younger, thinner, sexier.

Children in the UK spend 2,000 hours a year online, watching TV or playing computer games, compared with 900 hours in school.

So much time spent in front of so many screens. The derivatives market conjured into existence in the 1990s was a virtual world, enabling speculation not in real assets but in the risk of speculation itself. It *is* addictive: the rush, the buzz, the winning streak. The opposite of which is the losing nose-dive – lose your job and you're well on your way to losing your (real) house, marriage, health and dog.

£3.5 billion. Or do I mean trillion? Write it out, in figures. Draw smiley faces in the zeros. The mirror world of money, in which debts are packaged and repackaged and tied up with a pink ribbon bow and sold on: before I've drawn the last smile the zeros have multiplied. I start to feel dizzy; I need to lie down. Outside the bedroom window I can hear seagulls: how did *they* get here, so far inland?

If twelve fat cats can gobble £1 billion in four years, how long does it take Jack's dog to run a mile? Dick Fuld, CEO of Lehman Brothers at the time of its collapse in September 2008, when asked by the US Oversight Committee in Washington whether it was true he'd taken home $500 million over eight years, said, er, no, it was more like $300 million. John Thain of Merrill Lynch demanded a $10 million bonus in December 2008 after losing $5 billion in just three months; he spent $1.2 million on new fittings for his office (including a $1,400 waste basket) while his company was being bailed out. In the UK John Varley and Bob Diamond of Barclays together took home £50 million in four years. There's nothing to hold on to here: children are blowing bubbles through plastic hoops. But if we say one mile equals just £1 million and Jack's dog works at the current minimum wage (maybe at the gym where Fuld got punched in the face in October 2008) 35 hours a week with 20 days holiday a year, the answer is 104 years.

Wrong. Wrong question too. Jack's dog needs to get his bed and board sorted – which for a dog of reasonable intelligence in one of the richest countries in the world shouldn't be too difficult – but once he's done that he may not even *want* to run a mile. He may want to walk; he may want to read a book, sleep, write love letters to the bitch down the road, help other dogs with only three legs. He may want to just flop around in the park and chase a few seagulls. He can take as long as he likes.

Stendhal in 1835: 'To give any attention to money matters was deemed supremely low and contemptible in my family. To talk about money was somehow infra dig, money was a sad necessity, as it were, and its role alas indispensable, like that of the privy, but it was never to be spoken of.' He might be talking about the English middle classes in the 1950s.

For a very long time money, like sex, was something that happened behind closed doors; part of the pleasure lay in the secrecy. Then things changed. Both lust and greed were taken off the seven-deadly-sins list and re-categorised. Sex became fun, and if you weren't getting lots of it there must be something wrong with you. Money ditto. Stendhal's own indifference to money – 'The sight of a large sum of gold awakens no other thought in me than the bother of keeping it safe from thieves' – now seems quaint, other-worldly.

The consequences were many. James Buchan: 'For some time, and in many places, money was thought to be bad, but it is now thought, on the whole, to be good. That inversion is the greatest to have occurred in the moral sentiments of the West. Desires that resisted incorporation into money turned pale and lost their power to convince: disinterested friendship, love and philanthropy became as suspect as the goals of once passionate wishes, honour and salvation.'

But changes in attitude occur faster among some social groups than others; the idea of what is 'normal' (though still undefined by any EU regulation) and the anxiety involved in being compared to others are powerful restraints. Try asking your neighbour how much he earns, or how many lovers he's had. The same word –

obscene – is often used to describe both the salaries of CEOs/Premier League footballers and the kind of sex that isn't shown on the BBC.

The avant-garde, the swingers and fetish clubbers of the money revolution, were, of course, the investment bankers. Which is fine, except that it was your money and mine they were getting off on.

The home lives of bankers: is this a place we want to visit? An investment banker, quoted in the *Standard*: 'In most cases they know their wives despise them for enslaving their lives to money, and they know that the moment they lose their job their wives will walk and take the kids, and their £3 million home, and divorce them.' A lonely-hearts ad, placed on a literary website at the time the axe started to chop: 'Ex-banker, 33 . . . Seeking woman not interested in money, fast cars, champagne, holidays, fleecing innocent hard-working gullible twats, whilst telling them you love them. Bitch.' No, this is not a place I want to go. For all the gorgeous fixtures and fittings and the excellent wine. May the ex-bankers fare better.

The above house in Mayfair, London, was squatted in January 2009 by a group that offered free workshops on welding, yurt-building, bookbinding, song-writing and de-schooling society. Hundreds of buildings are squatted; what made the press interested in this one was the stark disparity between the poshness of the building (alleged to be worth £22.5 million) and the presumed poverty of the squatters. The world turned upside-down: as in those photographs of Saddam Hussein's hurriedly vacated palaces in Iraq in which the occupying US troops sprawl on the gilt sofas, play cards and slide down the marble banisters. Bookbinding and yurt-building won't change the world for the better overnight, but nor will sending out 400,000 repossession orders (Centre for Policy Studies estimate, February 2009) to households that have lost jobs and can't keep up the mortgage payments.

Do you bail out the car manufacturers and hasten the environmental catastrophe, or do you *not* bail them out and lose many thousands of jobs? Do you shoot yourself in the left foot or the right foot? I was pondering this while standing in the queue for tickets at the cinema with Jack's dog (Jack himself has sunk into depression, he rarely gets out of bed), and when I asked for his own opinion he tilted his head and asked: *Didn't you see this coming?* Well, yes, actually. I did. I reckon most of the audience did. You know when, sometime near the start of a film, there's a glamorous party with champagne flowing and everyone dancing into the night? There's no possible script that has all those people living happily ever after. And when you saw photos of the City wine bars at bonus time over the past several years, similar.

Just as we *know* we're fucking up the environment, and we're going to have to pay. Just as I *know* that some day I'm going to die. But this is a film that was passed with a PG certificate ('some scenes may be unsuitable for young children'), so nothing *really* nasty was going to happen; it was family-friendly, we were safe, we had nothing to worry about.

A bedtime story for Jack's dog. Say there's a banker – call her Jill – who, having bought one of the fancy packages because of the high percentage return promised on the pink ribbon, becomes curious about what's inside. She's alone in the office; the others have skipped off early to the wine bar. She unties the bow. Now begins a long and winding trail of paperwork that leads her, after many late nights straining her eyes over the small print, to the house that Jack built. She travels there – a few adventures to be added in here, showing her heartwarming awakening to life's realities – and finds a house now run-down, semi-derelict. She buys it. Jack comes home from work, smelling of monkey shit. Such are their names, they are meant for each other. The local vicar is offering wedding ceremonies at discount prices.

But, objects Jack's dog, she's too late. He's in love with his debt counsellor.

That's irrelevant, I tell him. When they come to make the movie, when all this is over, they'll cut out the debt counsellor or make her a small-town hysteric or a man. They're probably casting right now.

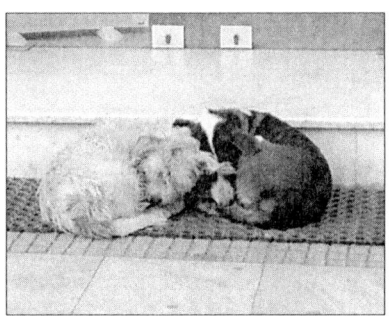

James Buchan: 'Money is one of those human creations that make concrete a sensation, in this case the sensation of wanting, as a clock does the sensation of passing time. It is that double aspect of money, airy and substantial, that has fascinated all civilisations . . . It seems to have a wandering or frontier reality, like a ghost or sailor who, to the ancient Greeks, seemed not wholly of the living or of the dead.'

Bollocks, says the man who taps me on the shoulder and asks me for 50p 'for a cup of tea', and Jack too and most people alive. But not the bankers. As they invented ever more complex financial instruments whose value derived from changes in anything from exchange rates to the weather, money became so airy that it lost all substantiality. Numbers rattling on a stock-exchange board. Electronic money. Invisible money. Imagined money. Until what they found they had was moneyless money.

And then? The banking system, because there appeared to be no alternative, was given life-support in the form of borrowing against the future, and thus itself now has 'a wandering or frontier reality'. And the bankers – it's hard to care, really, given how little care they took of us. But a few aspired themselves to the condition of being 'not wholly of the living or of the dead'. In January 2009 a US banker attempted to fake his own suicide by sending a distress call from his plane and then parachuting to the ground. In June 2008 another US banker vanished after leaving a suicide note on his abandoned car. 'Without a body,' said the state police investigator, 'we don't have conclusive evidence either way.'

*'The General Bank of Death
guarantees everything'*
— Gyorgy Petri, 'Credit Card'

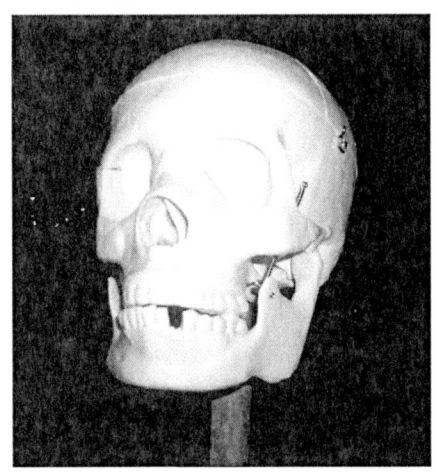

This plastic skull (made in China) was bought for a few quid in a joke shop. In 2007 Damien Hirst's platinum skull encrusted with 8,601 diamonds was sold for £50 million to 'an unnamed investor group'. 'Compared to the tearful sadness of a vanitas scene,' wrote the art historian Rudi Fuchs, 'the diamond skull is glory itself.' 'Among many things,' wrote Gordon Burn in 2008, 'it was the apotheosis of the recent inundation of liquidity into the art market.' The liquidity has been drying up, and a project for a group of unnamed investment bankers cut in half and preserved in formaldehyde remains unrealised.

'Missis and little 'uns a coming to keep you company?' asked the turnkey.

'Why, yes, we think it better that we should not be scattered, even for a few weeks.'

'Even for a few weeks, OF course,' replied the turnkey. And he followed him again with his eyes, and nodded his head seven times when he was gone.

The affairs of this debtor were perplexed by a partnership, of which he knew no more than that he had invested money in it; by legal matters of assignment and settlement, conveyance here and conveyance there, suspicion of unlawful preference of creditors in this direction, and of mysterious spiriting away of property in that; and as nobody on the face of the earth could be more incapable of explaining any single item in the heap of confusion than the debtor himself, nothing comprehensible could be made of his case. To question him in detail, and endeavour to reconcile his answers; to closet him with accountants and sharp practitioners, learned in the wiles of insolvency and bankruptcy; was only to put the case out at compound interest and incomprehensibility.

– Dickens, *Little Dorrit* (1855–7)

In 1914 they said the First World War would be over by Christmas. In November 2008 Alistair Darling said the British economy would return to growth in late 2009. The forecasts are beside the point (even when/if we move out of recession we'll still be in a depression). The country has borrowed so much that we are all now in Marshalsea debtors' prison indefinitely.

Dickens knew Marshalsea well: his father was imprisoned there in 1824 (for a debt of £40); to support his family, the twelve-year-old Dickens worked ten-hour shifts in a shoe-polish factory for 6 shillings a week. Debtors were housed three or four to a 10-foot-square room with a single bed and had to pay for their food; they remained there often for decades, with their families lodging with them (Little Dorrit herself is born in Marshalsea), unable to work yet denied their freedom until their debts had been paid off. Government regulation had little effect: the prison's two categories of inmates, debtors and smugglers, were supposed to be kept apart but in fact mingled freely – 'except at certain constitutional moments when somebody came from some Office, to go through some form of overlooking something which neither he nor anybody else knew anything about. On these truly British occasions, the smugglers, if any, made a feint of walking into the strong cells and the blind alley, while this somebody pretended to do his something: and made a reality of walking out again as soon as he hadn't done it – neatly epitomising the administration of most of the public affairs in our right little, tight little, island.' (*Little Dorrit*)

I had a dream in which I punched the keys to withdraw money from a cash machine and it paid out in cowrie shells, rattling down a metal chute into the canvas bag I'd thoughtfully brought with me. As I walked to the supermarket the shells clacked satisfyingly in the bag by my side – I felt rich, rich. And then I woke up and went to my real bank and there was nothing there for me at all, they'd completely run out of money. Not a bean.

She logs into her account and stares for ten minutes at the figures on the screen, waiting for the numbness to wear off. She calls the helpdesk. She listens to the menu, presses button two for current account holders and then button four for general inquiries, and is placed in a queue. Mozart is interrupted by a voice thanking her for her patience and by another offering her an upgrade to a premium account at discounted cost. She looks out of the window; it's a windless afternoon with the sound of traffic drifting up; in a flat on the opposite side of the street there is, suspiciously, someone else on the phone. Inderjit comes on the line and asks for various letters of her password and for the answer to her personal question, which turns out to be the name of her first pet, a brown-and-white dog that used to chew the edges of her father's books and was run over by a fire engine. What's the problem? 'I think I have been waiting for you,' she says, 'all my life', but Inderjit says he can't quite catch that and she asks him where all her money has gone? The line goes dead. She redials. Options, Mozart, messages, Mozart, security questions – this time from Dub, or Deb, who for the sake of keeping this short asks her straight off if she's calling about her overdraft limit.

No. Or yes. But first, where is her money? Her salary, for starters; her maintenance payments from her ex-husband. A lot of companies are having cash-flow problems, says Dub; he's probably lost his job, says Dub, who adds that she's lucky to have a job herself and by the way what is it? She is a debt counsellor. Pause, followed by hysterical laughter. OK, maybe in ten years' time she will be laughing herself but right now she is not in the mood. Asked why she hasn't taken advantage of the recommended anti-virus and personalisation features, she declares that the promise of freedom from such drivel – the freedom to 'be' herself, as the adverts had promised – was the very reason she signed up in the first place. Dub transfers her to another department in the person of Leila, who confirms the charges already made for exceeding her overdraft limit, spells out the interest accruing, and asks what she'd like to do about this. 'Cancel the last ten years of my life,' she suggests, and is transferred to Darren, who asks in a mellow Scots voice what underwear she is wearing: the fabric, the size, the colour, he needs everything. She puts the phone down. She remembers a boy she knew when she was about ten, a boy who once, in the middle of a wood, held up a handful of five-pound notes and set fire to them with a match. This was thrilling – and the boy looked, as he did this, like a priest officiating at a solemn rite – but it was confusing too, like some kind of test. That money, in those days, would have fed a family for a week, or paid their rent. She redials. Option two, option four, and then, astonishingly, silence. In her mind she sees – this was years ago, in Scotland – two bald men arm-wrestling at a table in a pub. There was a light sweat on the heads of both men, as there is now on her own face. Determined to outlast the imbecile on the other end of the line, who is being paid God knows how much an hour to wait until she puts the phone down first, she hangs on for several minutes until finally she is greeted by Asad, who is about seven years old. She asks to speak to, and after an interval enlivened by some African drumming is put through to, a supervisor. She explains bluntly to Mr Smith(?) that her life is not worthless, that besides working her guts out for twenty years she has raised three children, the future, and Mr Smith informs her that post-dated cheques are not acceptable. She sees that the room on the opposite side of the street is now empty. Where is he speaking from, she asks Mr Smith. He is not at liberty to say. She ponders this while wondering aloud if the accounts have got muddled and if the life that should have been hers is in fact being lived by someone else. Mr Smith assures her that the security and privacy of all accounts is an ongoing priority. All she wants, she says, is a new overdraft facility. Mr Smith recommends that she upgrade to a premium account – available for a limited period only at reduced rates – to give her access to an advanced helpdesk staffed by psychotherapists and ministers of all denominations. There are also, Mr Smith continues, lay members of this helpdesk democratically elected by all account holders, and as there happens right now to be a vacancy, perhaps she ... She laughs in his face, as much as you can do that down a phone line, and he asks her with extreme politeness to refrain from using abusive language and cuts her off. She drums her fingers on the table beside the phone, a habit she's only recently become aware of and which she dislikes, because she remembers as a child being irritated when her mother did this. Her mother, in fact, at around the time the dog went under the fire engine and her father's business went bankrupt, developed a number of odd habits: she wore the same clothes for a week or longer, she stopped preparing any meals except soup, which was served at odd times of the day, and she addressed every man who came to the door – the postman, the doctor, her cousin, even her husband – as Ben, the name of her brother; she seemed to be trying, if she could not altogether withdraw from life, to radically simplify it. *Our advisors are available 24 hours a day, seven days a week, to assist you.* She has no money. She has less than no money. She will be buried in a pauper's grave. As was – can this be true? – Mozart. She tries to remember if there is any white wine left in the fridge or if she finished the bottle last night. *Press the star key if you want to hear these options again.* She is hopeful about that wine, just as she is hopeful that her ex-husband will get another job, though this is unlikely, and that her children will not have to go to school without shoes. She thinks of the shoes that she was going to buy for herself at the end of the month and now won't. *We apologise for keeping you waiting.* If she were a hermit, she thinks, as her mother would have preferred to be, there would be no one around to see her wearing those shoes, but she would still put them on, on special days that would be entirely of her own choosing. *Calls may be monitored or recorded for training purposes.* Outside, the sun is going down behind the block of flats in which she is living, and a swarm of starlings gusts upwards from the trees below her window. I am in a loop, she thinks, watching the swivelling flight of the birds, and suddenly has a dizzy feeling that she is travelling at great speed. She raises her arm to her mouth and bites herself, hard. Then she reaches again for the phone, but before she dials she has a flashback to this morning, when she was walking down to the shops and in front of her, sitting on the pavement with his legs splayed in front of him, was a man wearing a fluorescent yellow jacket and a woollen hat. It looked like he'd been there for some time. He was a big man, a heavy man; he'd need to lean to one side and press down with his hand on the pavement when he wanted to stand up; and if anyone bent down to speak to him there'd be a pause before he answered. As she passed him and then when she turned to look back she saw that he'd got in his lap the end of a cable pulled up from a hole in the pavement and he was fiddling about with a jumble of tiny coloured wires. He was a telephone engineer, that's who he was. But he appeared to be sorting through his intestines, with great concentration and skill, even though his hands, like his whole body, were big and chubby. She had thought, this morning, that if she ever needed cutting open and her own intestines sorting out, or whatever else was inside her – a situation not at all unlikely, though she hadn't realised at the time how imminent it was – she would trust that man to do it. Foolishly, and absolutely.

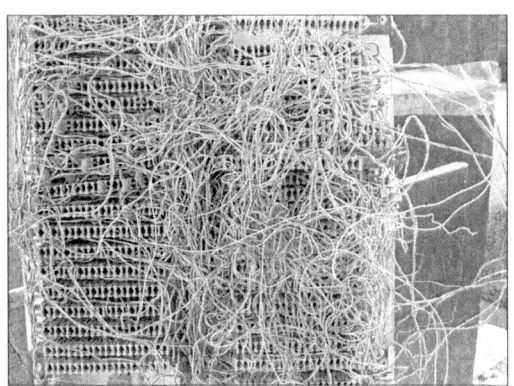

Here is an iron-foundry worker in 1955 being presented with a clock in recognition of his long service. Clocking in, clocking out, and after twenty-five years he gets given a clock. Once, aged three or four, I was hefted up onto my father's shoulders and taken into that foundry – the blackness, the fiery furnace – and I screamed to be let down. It's possible I misremember, but there's no one around now to confirm or refute. It's a long time ago, another world. Britain was a manufacturing and industrial country then; now, 'services' (a large part of which, at least until last year, was 'financial services') account for 73 per cent of the GDP. Then, black-and-white, jobs for life and – no need for nostalgia – a rigid class system and casual, everyday racism. Now, high-definition colour, hot-desking, and a general loosening up in social relations. But it's not *that* long ago. Squatting on some mantelpiece, the clock in the photograph may still be ticking. And still, when I go into almost any workplace – with its line-managers and performance-related pay and reserved parking for the bosses – I scream to be let out.

The dignity of labour? In most work done by most people there's no dignity at all: it's bland, repetitive, pointless. But because of this, there's something else: an unsung, unheroic heroism. Five days a week, in fair weather and foul, for forty years of their lives or longer, men and women set off in the morning for some un-lovely factory/office/shop/building site and put in the hours – a means to an end, the end being the paying of bills and the upkeep of a home in which they can raise the next generation to enter the cycle.

'A crowd flowed over London Bridge, so many . . .'

And when they are laid off, kicked out, *let go*, they can phone the UK Insolvency Helpline for 'free, independent and impartial debt advice'.

Before his first drink on his first date with Jane, his debt counsellor, Jack's male self-esteem is not high: he has stood before her financially naked, exposing his puny income and all his arrears, every debt and overdraft charge and unpaid fine and all the accumulated interest, and it was not a pretty sight. She didn't blanch. She made lists, in columns, and tapped figures on a calculator. She had small hands, delicate fingers. By his second drink Jack knows that her husband left her five years ago with three hungry children and a heap of unpaid bills and she's been though all this herself, who hasn't. By his third drink she's become the most attractive female he's met for years. Ordering his fourth drink, Jack knows that she's right, that a deal can be worked out, that everything will be taken care of. On his fifth drink Jack suddenly sees who they really are – they are Bonnie and Clyde, pitched against the system and forever in love, so adored by the public that the traffic parts to let them through as they accelerate away with the swag from the bank.

Ou sont les magasins d'antan? As well as the big ones, the small ones too. The place at the end of the road where I used to get my shoes re-heeled – where did that go? The café with over-priced food but a garden at the back where I could smoke? The minicab office in the next street? With the deadpan Somali driver who'd stop the car and get out and look up at the sky: he said he navigated by the stars, and I never knew whether he was taking the piss. Even with no office to return to, I hope that somewhere he's still driving. There are very few recession-proof businesses; here is one of them.

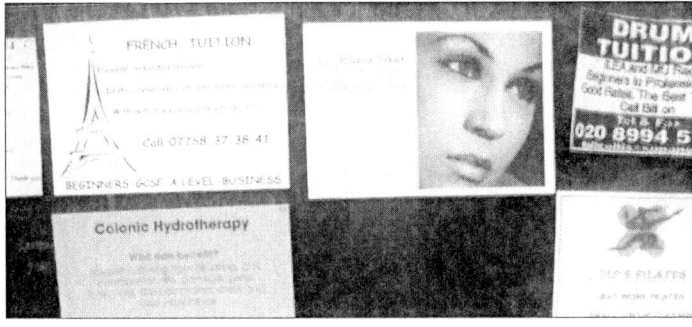

In good times, French lessons, beauty treatments, drumming tuition and pilates are, along with Sky Plus and holidays in Santorini, what surplus income gets spent on. In bad times, the non-essentials get cut: Betsy the pet rabbit gets driven to the outskirts and not brought back, and it's crossed Jack's mind to do likewise with his dog. What other frills can we do without? *Not* colonic hydrotherapy: this is exactly what the banking system needs, to flush out the toxic debt. ('After your colonic irrigation procedure,' advises the NHS, 'you may be given some probiotics, which contain beneficial bacteria that help to keep your digestive system healthy. The probiotics may either be inserted into your rectum, or taken as tablets.') But there are still many luxuries we can cut. In March the monarchy was put up for sale – there are other countries fonder of the royals than we are, and this was a quality export product. Up for offers along with the monarchy was this fine collection (opposite) of second-hand flagpoles.

That man behind the arras – Polonius? That spoilsport, irritant, pedantic old fool. 'Neither a borrower nor a lender be.' He got killed off in Act 3, a quick rapier thrust. Never one of the main actors; a bit-part player. Now, what was that he was on about?

Money grows on trees, like birds: here on wintry branches are the little boxes in which it incubates and hatches.

Global warming has severely affected breeding habits and migration routes.

People used to believe you could *make* money by hard work, but nowadays even small children have watched enough television to see through that old tale.

It's odourless. It doesn't bite. Its call is monotonous. But golly it skips around, isn't there when you want it. Fickle, like all the gods. It was supposedly domesticated many thousands of years ago but so were horses and when you look into their eyes you know that isn't quite true.

The intensive factory farming of money makes it prone to many diseases, some of which can be transmitted to humans.

There are government regulations concerning the application of biotechnology to the breeding of money, and there are also ways around them.

In the last fifty years that part of the human brain dedicated to devising ways of getting money away from others and into your own hands has increased in size by 4 per cent.

Below are simple mobile sieves provided by supermarkets: money flows through the holes, and you are left with a packet of cornflakes, a jar of anti-wrinkle cream and half a dozen tins of dogfood.

It's late.

Everyone feels this, after a certain age. Very possibly the lateness of the hour is something people have always felt, whatever their age and whatever age they were living in. I'm pretty sure that my forebears in the Middle Ages didn't feel they were living in the *middle*, and in the run-up to the year AD 1000 many of them believed the world was about to end. 'Perdition and extinction' was how Max Nordau, in the cheery way that intellectuals have, characterised the mood at the end of the 19th century.

Still, it's late. We've finished the wine and the jokes are getting blacker. The planet is heating up, species are dying out, we'll soon be fighting wars over not just petrol but water. So many of the bright ideas of the last century ended up in blood-soaked ditches that anyone suggesting a new one is reckoned simple-minded. And now this recession mess, which shows we can't even do simple maths.

But there are children sleeping upstairs, and in the morning they'll come to wake us up with their breezy voices and their sunny and expectant eyes.

He fell down the stairs. He slipped on the ice. He was coming home from work on Friday night when he got mugged – they took his money, his cards, his identity papers. They flung back his wallet, empty except for the photo of his kids – his kids to whom he'll say, on Saturday morning, that he fell down the stairs, that he slipped on the ice.

What are banks *for*? – (a) a safer place for your cash than under the mattress; (b) profits for bankers and investors; (c) to provide credit for new and growing businesses; (d) meeting attractive strangers while you're waiting in the queue; (e) to enable a general and sustainable increase in prosperity throughout society; or (f) all of the above (in which case, list in order of priority)?

In 2008 the first branch of the Grameen Bank opened in New York. It lends money to poor people with no current bank account, no credit history, no collateral, no guarantors. Co-founded in 1983 by Muhammad Yunus (Nobel Peace Prize, 2006), the Grameen Bank had by late 2008 lent around $7 billion to 7.5 million borrowers in Bangladesh, more than 90 per cent of them women, and 64 per cent of its borrowers had moved from below the wavery grey mark known as the poverty line to above it. The bank's repayment rate is 98 per cent: no need for bailing out. Micro-credit for the poor to get themselves out of being poor, and no one loses.

The doors of the bank on the opposite page are still open and the traffic lights are working too. When banks fail, so much else goes down too. The traffic lights above were owned by a bank with a sideline in charging wealthy drivers for the lights to turn green, and offering loans for in-car entertainment systems for the poorer drivers who got stuck in long queues. The bank closed, and now the traffic lights function only as a message board for dogs.

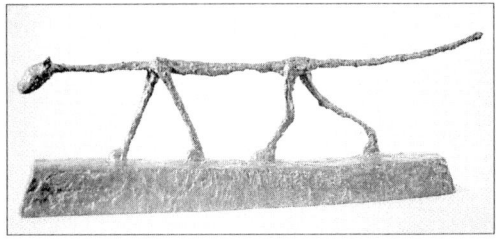

Giacometti: inside every fat cat is a thin cat struggling to get out.

When you dig up the road – to rewire the traffic lights, to start reconstructing the banks – it's not a pretty sight. There are skeletons down there, worms, rats, things you don't want to know about (and things you really should know about but others would prefer you didn't). Old bones buried by Jack's dog and then forgotten. Contaminated soil. *Roots*. Not for the first time you think it would really be much easier to start again from scratch, but that's not an option. You put your hand down – through the the rubble, the mud, the squelch – children would love this – and grab hold of something covered in slime and bring it to the surface and think, Jesus, what do I do with *this*?

Tea break. Did you hear the one about the investment banker and the headless chicken? Did you hear the one about the workmen who were digging up the *wrong road*?

Behind this door – which is in a yard in the City of London – is the secret meeting place of a group of underground bankers. (There's no external handle; you have to whisper the password through the grille on the right.) This group is deeply suspect: they buy books and music, not yachts and ski chalets, and their vocabulary extends beyond that of company reports. They are regarded by the rest of the banking world as heretics – because the whole point of being a banker is to speak in clichés, to have a single-track mind, to buy only the most predictable goods: that way they remain anonymous, almost invisible, and are left alone to get on with their thing.

Or else: the yachts/ski chalets are a front and the bankers are in fact revolutionary Marxists who have engineered the whole fiasco to hasten the end of capitalism. Or else: the books/music of the secret fraternity are also a front, and in fact this lot are ten times more financially focused and savvy than the others (not hard) and are the only ones who are going to come out of this in profit.

Item 26: democracy. The export manager reported a slump in sales. Was it priced too high? The chairman wondered where all the women disappeared to – 'Where are *they* when you open the box?' The production manager admitted that the fit between 'the people' and the other bit called 'free market' seemed a bit loose, as if there was a part missing. The IT manager said something about compatibility. The head of sales wondered if the time was right to develop a cheaper, more streamlined model. The acting publicity director said yes, yes, and she was sure she could get a couple of A-list celebs for the ads. The financial director said that funding wasn't available for a full R&D programme and suggested that the boys and girls in marketing might take a look at the packaging. The chairman said that his favourite colour was blue.

In the open spaces of the shopping mall, story-tellers try to catch your eye. All their stories are sad: they are about abused or starving children, animals destroyed in scientific experiments, journalists and students imprisoned and tortured because they're unlucky enough to live under some one-truth-fits-all regime. Photographs and documents are produced: like the sales people in expensive clothes shops, the story-tellers are concerned to demonstrate that their wares are the real thing. Unlike everything else in the mall, the stories are free, but if you are moved by them the story-teller will expect you to offer money. Now it gets tricky: you yourself have to decide how much the stories are worth. You open your wallet. You are a good person, but how good? You recall how the quote from Wallace Shawn on page 1 goes on: 'Everyone knows that the world will not do everything today.'

God is dead (so can't bail us out). Or couldn't afford the heating bills for a place this big, or had had it up to here with the regular early-hours racket outside the lap-dancing club at the end of the street. Whatever the reason, he's gone. But he left no forwarding address, so the mail just keeps piling up inside the door.

'*Grow edible microscopic organisms in lakes. Every lake will become a kettle of ready-made soup that needs only to be heated. Contented people will lie about on the shores, swimming and having dinner.*'

The above is the first of thirty 'Proposals' published in Moscow in 1915 by Velimir Khlebnikov, who was writing in one of those brief periods in history when people truly believe they can design and build a better world. This is number two: '*Effect the exchange of labour and services by means of an exchange of heartbeats. Estimate every task in terms of heartbeats – the monetary unit of the future, in which all individuals are equally wealthy.*' Mad, you may think; but really it's no more insane than certain other ways of running the economy.

He slipped the lead. He couldn't take it – the bickering, the silences, the head-in-hands slump. Jack's hours at the zoo were cut but not the monkey shit so he left the cages unlocked and the monkeys vanished, his job too. Down on their uppers, they squabbled (like seagulls!), Jack and his live-in debt counsellor, the fine Jane. They tried the Bonnie-and-Clyde thing: they drove off, parked outside the bank, went for a drink to get their courage up, came out of the pub to find the car had been clamped. Or the other version: they drove off, gun in his pants, and a mile out of town the petrol gauge was showing zero. Neither of them had money. No problem, says Jack, we'll fill up on the way out. On the *getaway*? Jane says. We tell the cops to take a *coffee break* while we fill up with petrol? They argued, she reached for the wheel and they slewed into a ditch and bashed a telephone pole. No insurance. Either way, they walked home. Jane's children came back from school and they were hungry and curious. What's for tea? Why can't I pee and sneeze at the same time? Why can't they just print more banknotes and give them to people? With the curiosity, with learning how the world fits together, Jack's dog was helpful; about the hunger he could do nothing. He had hoped that as capitalism imploded those elements of a decent human life that resisted reckoning in monetary value – friendship, leisurely breakfasts, long hot baths, helping others – would re-assert themselves. When everyone went to bed early (the bailiffs had taken the TV) he read aloud to them from both Karl ('The essence of money is not primarily that it externalises property, but that the mediating activity or process – the human and social act in which man's products reciprocally complement one another – becomes alienated and takes on the quality of a material thing, money, external to man. By externalising this mediating activity, man is active only as he is lost and dehumanised') and Groucho Marx ('A child of five would understand this. Send someone to fetch a child of five'). But money is never so real as when you haven't got it, when you are mocked by the needs and desires it's not there to translate. Jane was on antidepressants. Jack bought meat from the back door of a supermarket – by now everything tasted of cardboard anyway – and coughed blood for a week. They blamed the bankers, then they blamed each other, then they blamed themselves, then they blamed each other even more viciously. They made up, fucked, looked out of the window and sulked. The children moped, cried, drew cave-paintings on the walls with strawberry jam. There's a limit. So exit dog. Not far – he's around, this dog, biding time, Jack believes, unwilling to give up on the bond that's there between a man and his beast.

Toad/Goodwin had a point when he said (page 12) that it was too simple to blame the whole mess on the bankers. The politicians who gave them the nod and a fair few knighthoods too? The developers who got fat on soaring property prices, the investors chasing ever higher returns? Everyone who slept with the enemy? Still, when the pension cheques get sent out to the early-retired bankers, no reason not to put in the envelopes a copy of Plutarch's account of the death of Brutus: 'Grasping with both hands his naked sword by the hilt, he fell upon it.'

Two hot, stifling summer afternoons in America:

The first is in 1922 in New York. *'But it's so hot,' insisted Daisy, on the verge of tears, 'and everything's so confused. Let's all go to town.'* They hire a room in the Plaza Hotel – Daisy, Tom, Gatsby, Jordan and Nick – where 'opening the windows admitted only a gust of hot shrubbery from the Park' and they bicker about a man called Biloxi and whether Gatsby is really an Oxford man and whether Daisy ever really loved Tom, even when she married him, and then they get back in their cars and drive back to Long Island, killing Tom's mistress on the way.

'Her voice is full of money,' says Gatsby of Daisy – Daisy, 'gleaming like silver, safe and proud above the hot struggles of the poor'.

The second hot, hot afternoon is on a Sunday in 1936. The Depression rules. James Agee is driving out from Birmingham, Alabama, to the sharecroppers whose lives he will record. In the empty streets of a township 'a small hound took the street, trying to go slow because he felt slow and was born slow, but using his feet staccato because the pavement hurt them. It was as hot as all the days of the week piled one on top of another, or as if they were a series of small burning-glasses . . .' Heat-struck, he thinks of a woman ('but she must not be a whore or a bitch, nor any girl I knew well either, but a girl nearly new to me') and of death ('I could twist the car off the road, if possible into a good-sized oak, and the chances are fair that I would kill myself, and I don't care much about doing that either'). He comes across the Ricketts children, and then Ricketts himself, who as a wind rises leads him to the house of George Gudger, 'expectant of storm, the dust sunken about it like sucked-back smoke of magic, the plants released erect and trembling as flesh at the end of shock of surgery, the house quiet save one blind creaking, a bull waiting the hammer'. The storm breaks, 'a grey roar that runs out of the woods behind your house and takes the field in a stride'. They go inside and shelter in a room 'in near dead darkness, in which at first I know, only, that it is full of people, whom I do not yet see'. Gradually, in the light that comes through cracks in the walls and roof 'in short lead slivers', and then when a kerosene lamp is lit, he makes out children, women, other men, and as they wait out the storm there is in their glances, snatches of talk, small movements and gestures, a richness 'much beyond what I can set down'. Eventually the rain ceases, and he is among people 'who find themselves resumed each into his ordinary being, before he is quite ready to reassume it'. They sort peaches from a tree the storm has split in half. He drives Ricketts home, then on the way back to the highway manages to sink the car in mud. He walks to the Gudgers' place, is taken in, fed, offered the bed the children have been sleeping in. After a fitful night interrupted by the attentions of bedbugs and lice he is woken before dawn by Gudger: it's Monday, there's work to be done.

'I sat in the steep-tilted car maybe a full minute with the motor idling, feeling a smile all over the bones of my face as strange to me as greasepaint.'

Highgate cemetery, London, is the kind of place where Jack's dog may be loitering, somewhere between the tombs of Karl Marx (1818–83) and George Wombwell (1777–1850), lion tamer and menagerie exhibitor. What the bourgeoisie produces, Marx argues in *The Communist Manifesto*, is 'its own grave-diggers'.

References

page 10: Adam Zagajewski, 'Apes', *Canvas* (1991)

11: 'They need a cigar': *Guardian*, 6 February 2009

13: Goodwin: the squabble over his pension was still going on when this book was printed. RBS's takeover of NatWest in 2000, guided by Goodwin, resulted in the loss of 18,000 jobs (*Independent*, 14 October 2008);
dogfights and Socialist Lunatic: John Preston, 'Kenneth Grahame: lost in the wild wood', *Daily Telegraph*, 8 February 2008

13 (and others): James Buchan, *Frozen Desire: An Inquiry into the Meaning of Money* (1997)

14: Children in the UK: *The Times*, 21 January 2009, quoting *Consumer Kids* by Ed Mayo and Agnes Nairn (2009)

17: Fuld punched: *Daily Telegraph*, 7 October 2008

18: Stendhal, *The Life of Henry Brulard* (1836; 1995)

20: an investment banker: *Evening Standard* magazine, 9 January 2009; lonely-hearts ad: untitledbooks.com

24: a US banker: *Evening Standard*, 14 January 2009; another US banker: usnews.com, 11 June 2008

25: Gyorgy Petri, 'Credit Card', *Eternal Monday* (1999);
Rudi Fuchs: whitecube.com/exhibitions/beyond_belief;
Gordon Burn: *Born Yesterday: The News as a Novel* (2008)

51: Velimir Khlebnikov, 'Proposals' (1915–16), in *Collected Works of Velimir Khlebnikov*, vol. 1, trans. Paul Schmidt (1987)

53: Karl Marx, 'Money and Alienated Man' (1844), in *Writings of the Young Marx on Philosophy and Society* (1997)

55: F. Scott Fitzgerald, *The Great Gatsby* (1925). Nick is a bond salesman; Gatsby has 'phantom millions'.

56: James Agee, *Let Us Now Praise Famous Men* (1941)

Thanks to Wiesiek for the photos on pages 8, 9. 10 (lower), 19, 23, 29, 51; and to FreeDigitalPhotos.net for the toad on page 12. The photo on page 7 was clipped from a newspaper several years ago; it's possible the man is not a banker at all and is kind to small animals.

Essential reading: 'Jump! You Fuckers!', essay by Dan Hind, January 2009 (available on the Verso website: versobooks.com/books/ghij/h-titles/hind_d_threat_reason.shtml).

CB editions

01 / Erik Houston *The White Room*
02 / Jennie Walker *24 for 3*
03 / Jack Robinson *Days and Nights in W12*
04 / Stefan Grabiński *In Sarah's House*
    (translated by Wiesiek Powaga)
05 / *Saxon* screenplay by Greg Loftin
06 / Gert Hofmann *Lichtenberg & The Little Flower Girl*
    (translated by Michael Hofmann)
07 / Francis Ponge *Unfinished Ode to Mud*
    (translated by Beverley Bie Brahic)
08 / Elise Valmorbida *The TV President*
09 / Andrzej Bursa *Killing Auntie and Other Work*
    (translated by Wiesiek Powaga)
10 / J. O. Morgan *Natural Mechanical*
11 / Christopher Reid *The Song of Lunch*
12 / Jack Robinson *Recessional*

www.cbeditions.com